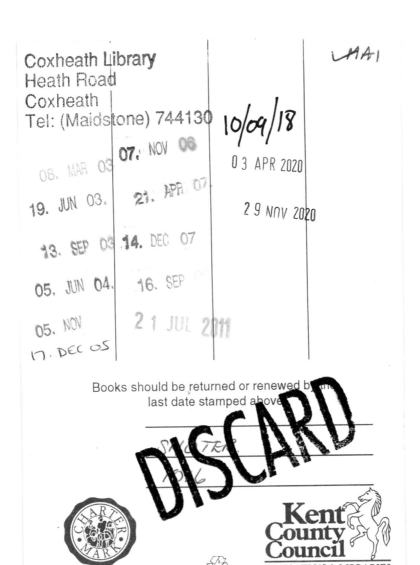

A CeNTuRy
OF CHANGE

Space and Technology

Jane Shuter

Heinemann
LIBRARY

First published in Great Britain by Heinemann Library,
Halley Court, Jordan Hill, Oxford OX2 8EJ
a division of Reed Educational and Professional
Publishing Ltd.
Heinemann is a registered trademark of Reed Educational
& Professional Publishing Ltd.

OXFORD MELBOURNE AUCKLAND
JOHANNESBURG BLANTYRE GABORONE
IBADAN PORTSMOUTH (NH) USA CHICAGO

Designed by Celia Floyd
Originated by Ambassador
Printed in Hong Kong/China

03 02 01 00 99
10 9 8 7 6 5 4 3 2 1

ISBN 0 431 03880 5

British Library Cataloguing in Publication Data

Shuter, Jane
    Space and Technology. – (A century of change)
    1. Technology – Great Britain – History – 19th
      century – Juvenile literature
    2. Technology – Great Britain – History – 20th
      century – Juvenile literature
    3. Outer space – Exploration – History – Juvenile
      literature
    I. Title
    629'.09

Acknowledgements

The Publishers would like to thank the following for
permission to reproduce photographs:

British Film Institute, p. 16; e.t. archive, p. 18; Mary
Evans Picture Library, pp. 4, 6, 10, 26; NASA, p. 5;
Nikon, p. 15; NOVOSTI, pp. 22, 24; Robert Harding
Picture Library, p. 13; Science Museum/Science and
Society Picture Library, pp. 8, 12, 14, 20, 25; Science
Photo Library, pp. 7, 9, 11, 19, 21, 23, 27, 28, 29;
Touchstone/Amblin (courtesy Kobal)

Cover photograph reproduced with permission of Science
and Society Picture Library and NASA/Science Photo
Library.

Our thanks to Becky Vickers for her help in the
preparation of this book.

Every effort has been made to contact copyright holders
of any material reproduced in this book. Any omissions
will be rectified in subsequent printings if notice is given
to the Publisher.

For more information about Heinemann Library books,
or to order, please telephone +44 (0)1865 888066, or
send a fax to +44 (0)1865 314091. You can visit our
website at www.heinemann.co.uk

Any words appearing in the text in bold, **like this**, are
explained in the glossary.

CONTENTS

Technology

Technology is the use of tools, power and materials to make something. Humankind has always used tools, from the stone axes of prehistoric times to the robots and computers of today. In the 100 years from 1900 to 2000, tools, and the technologies used to create them, have changed almost beyond belief.

This painting done in 1897 shows the gas lamps being lit on the Thames Embankment in London.

Power and progress

In 1900 most homes and businesses still did not have electricity supplies. Candles, oil and gas gave most people their light and most cooking was done burning wood or coal although gas stoves were becoming popular.

At the beginning of the century space travel did not seem possible. The technology did not exist to get people into space – they had only just conquered the air. The first aeroplane flight was in 1903.

Power and progress

Today electricity is used all over the world. It powers everything from home appliances to complex **electronic** music systems. Cheap, clean and abundant power has pushed forward technological development by providing the energy needed to run the tools of today.

New materials

New technologies not only need sources of energy. Some advances, like electronics and fibre optics, needed new materials to push forward technology. From film used in movies to the **silicon chips** used in microprocessors, development of new materials has boosted technological advances.

Blast off!

The most spectacular technological advances during the twentieth century have taken place in the area of space travel. Electronics, superfuels, and new strong, lightweight materials have all played a part in propelling humans into the air and then out into space. As well as space travel, advances in telescope technology have let scientists see into the furthest reaches of our universe to witness the birth, life and death of distant stars.

The *Venture Star* is the latest in reuseable space shuttles.

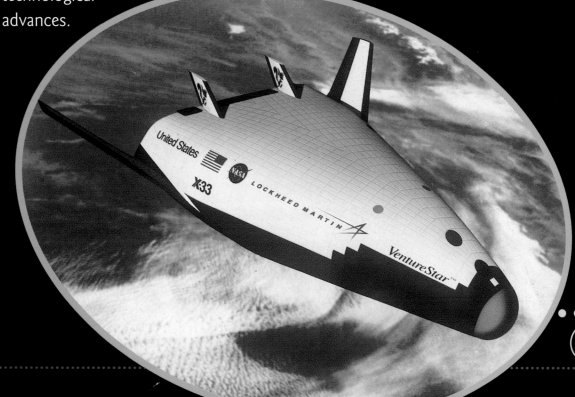

The first transmission of electrical power from place to place on overhead **conductors** only took place in 1873. By 1881, in New York City, Thomas Edison had opened the first electric power generating and distribution system. From that moment the world seemed to go power crazy. Private homes were wired up for electric light. Factories started changing over to this new source of energy rather than using their own **generators**.

AC or DC?

The new coal-fired electric power generators could produce two kinds of electric current, **alternating current (AC)** or **direct current (DC)**. Power stations that generated both kinds were set up. By 1900 AC current was the most widely used.

What to electrify next?

By 1900 it was possible to send messages electrically using **telegraph** and telephone systems.

Albin MICHEL
ÉDITEUR
22, rue Huyghens, 22
PARIS (14°)

ABONNEMENTS :
FRANCE...... 12 francs
ÉTRANGER.. 18 francs

LE PETIT INVENTEUR

LES DANGERS DE L'ÉLECTRICITÉ

L'électricité, si pratique et si avantageuse, présente cependant quelques réels dangers, si on l'emploie sans précautions dans des circonstances particulières, dont vous trouverez ici l'énumération.

Electricity powered lights, trams and some railways. It ran factory machines and powered lifts. In 1901 Hubert Cecil Booth introduced his electrical invention that would help with housework for many years to come – the electric vacuum cleaner.

This French cartoon from 1928 shows the fears that many people had about electricity to begin with.

Today electricity is still widely used, but there are now many new ways of generating it. Research into **renewable** forms of generating power will become more and more important as the old energy-generating fuels become more scarce. There is also a growing need for **pollution-**free sources of power.

Water power

From the earliest times, humans have harnessed the power of water, but during the 20th century huge **hydro-electric power** projects, using high-technology dam engineering with computer controls, have been built around the world. In most parts of the world, hydro-electric power (HEP) is the cheapest and cleanest way to generate electricity.

Sun and wind

The sun and wind can be used to generate electricity with very little pollution. Solar panels gather energy from the sun to use as a power source, and wind farms with special windmills to generate electricity have been built. But they are not always reliable – sunshine and wind do not appear every day.

Nuclear power

Nuclear power was a **by-product** of the development of the atomic bomb during World War II. By the late 1950s it was growing as a cheap and efficient way of producing electric power. But the dangers of this 'miracle' power gradually became obvious. The waste material produced by nuclear power plants was bad for the environment. Any leaks of **radioactive** materials could be dangerous to the environment and people. Accidents, like equipment failure or explosions, could cause contamination and death.

This solar energy site is in the Mojave Desert of California, USA. There are 650,000 computer-controlled mirrors that follow the sun across the sky. The site generates 275 megawatts of electricity.

In 1900 there were machines, like the comptometer, that did some mathematical calculations. They used a simple binary language on punch cards. A binary language uses a pattern of on–off signalling to create all of its instructions. It was first successfully used in 1805 by Frenchman Joseph Jacquard to give pattern instructions to weaving looms. Punch cards were fed into the machine to create the design. If there was a hole in the card the thread moved position; if there was no hole the thread stayed in the same position.

Analytical engine

In 1835 in England, Charles Babbage invented what he called an 'Analytical Engine'. This machine was really the first **digital** computer, because it used punch cards with an on–off binary code (hole, no hole) to work. The Analytical Engine was never completed. After his death it was forgotten until his notebooks and plans came to light in 1937.

Data processing

In 1886 an American statistician, Herman Hollerith, was sorting out the information from the 1880 US **census**. He realized that he could use the Jacquard loom card system to sort the information that was taking him so long to do by hand. He made a machine that used cards with holes to complete an electric circuit. If there was no hole, then the circuit could not be completed and the information was not entered. His machine sorted the information from the 1890 US census three times faster than the 1880 census, despite the fact that it had to deal with more information.

The comptometer was a very early calculator.

The computer revolution

The computers of today are smaller, lighter, faster and can do much more than the crude mathematical computation machines of 1900. They no longer need punch cards because they use **silicon chip** microprocessors instead. These microprocessors are made up of thousands of tiny components called **capacitors**. Computers are now used everywhere – in schools, shops, offices, hospitals and the home.

Storing information in computer mega-brains

In the 1950s, information downloaded from computers was stored on large reels of magnetic tape. Then floppy disks were invented. They, too, stored information magnetically but could store much more in a smaller space. In the 1980s compact discs (CDs) were first used to store information. They use **laser** technology and can store more than 300 times as much information as a floppy disk. They also can store high quality pictures, moving images and sound.

Operating systems

Computers use special programs called operating systems to run. Over the last 50 years these have become more user-friendly. Because it is so much easier to use computers, people who are not experts, sometimes with no knowledge or understanding of how computers work, can use computers in their jobs or for fun. Bill Gates and his company Microsoft have led the revolution in simplifying computer systems for use by non-experts.

Today's computers can be used for many things, such as browsing the Internet or playing games.

Steam power

In 1900 factories used machinery to make goods, from bicycles to textiles. The machinery was mainly powered by steam. Factories had largely replaced the system of producing goods by hand at home or in small workshops. Because factories were at least partly **mechanized** and usually larger than workshops, they were quicker, cheaper and more efficient. They also used a method first introduced in 1798 by the American inventor Eli Whitney – the **assembly line**.

In 1904 it took 12 hours to produce a Ford car. In 1913 mass production was introduced. By 1920 the time was 1 minute per car.

Mass production

The car industry in the early 1900s introduced the next big change in factory working – the mass production assembly line. For example, cars were first produced one at a time, with workers doing several different jobs. In mass production, making a car was broken down into stages. The cars moved along a conveyor belt with workers each doing a single, small, job on each car, over and over. This made production quicker – workers only had one job to learn and special tools to hand. So more cars could be produced and sold more cheaply. The work was more boring than making a whole car.

Changing factories

In 1900 the main goods produced in factories were cloth, iron, steel, and railway and ship parts. Today, while these things are still made, factories have to meet different needs. People want things that had not even been invented in 1900, such as, vehicle parts, computers, telecommunications goods and aeroplanes. These are the goods factories produce the most of in modern times.

There are also many 'white coat' factories making computer parts, food products, medical goods, chemicals and **pharmaceuticals**. These factories need to be absolutely sterile. No contamination can be brought in on the workers' bodies or clothing, so they have to change into special clean uniforms, shoes and hats at work.

Robot workers

Many factories where the same job has to be done over and over again have managed to automate their assembly lines. This means that less people are needed to do the same work. This has led to fewer people being employed on the factory floor. Workers are still needed to run the business and service the machines, but automation has caused unemployment in the assembly line industries, such as car manufacturing.

This factory in Japan uses robots to weld car bodies together. The factory still has to employ human workers to keep the machines running and to check the cars.

11

If people wanted to listen to music in 1900 they either sang or played instruments themselves or went to see live performances. It was possible to record music or the human voice, but the recordings were very poor quality and few people could afford the expensive equipment needed for recording and play-back.

These gramophone records were cheaper to make and made louder sounds because they could be played back using hard needles. Each recording still only played for a few minutes. But by 1900 the gramophone was the most popular system being used.

Cylinder or disc?

The phonograph was the first recording device. It was invented in 1877 by American Thomas Edison. Using large horn-shaped cylinders to catch the sounds, it then recorded them by making dents on thin sheets of tin foil, wrapped around a cylinder. By 1887 most recordings were being made onto wax cylinders, which were softer, so the recordings were clearer. In the same year, in the USA, Emile Berliner invented a way of making recordings onto flat spiral-grooved discs.

A gramophone with a disc on the turntable. The sound came from the big horn.

Today, modern technology can produce very high quality sound. It is louder, clearer and more true to life.

Laser technology

From the early 1980s, a new method of recording became possible – the plastic compact disc (CD). Sound is recorded onto a CD by a **laser** beam cutting a spiral of small pits at different levels into the plastic. In a CD player, the CD is scanned by another laser beam as it spins, which reflects light back from the non-pitted parts of the disc. The reflections of light from the CD are read by a light sensor and turned into electrical signals. The signals are then turned back into sound waves. Unlike vinyl records and magnetic tapes, CDs do not need to be touched by any mechanical equipment such as a needle when played, so they are less likely to get damaged.

Woofers and tweeters

A hundred years ago the loudspeaker on Edison's phonograph was huge and horn-shaped. Today, modern technology has created compact loudspeakers that are quite different. They can recreate sound from electrical signals very accurately.

Using coils of wire and magnets, the changing signals are converted into sound. Very good quality, high-fidelity (hi-fi) speakers need three different kinds of loudspeaker in the same unit to deal with different sound **frequencies**. The part that the deep, low sounds are played through is called a woofer. The middle sounds come out through a squawker and the highest notes are reproduced by a tweeter. Speakers still have small, horn-shaped cones inside them to spread the sound out.

Each CD has at least 3 billion tiny pits spiralled through the plastic. The spiral track within a 12-cm CD is more than 5 km long. The laser in a CD player reads the signals off the CD at a rate of 20,000 per second.

The first photographs were daguerreotypes, named after their inventor Louis-Jacques-Mande Daguerre. Daguerreotypes were shown in Paris in 1838–39. During the 1900s photography became a craze. Inventors worked hard to find the quickest, cheapest easiest methods. The winner was George Eastman in the USA. In 1888 he produced a cheap, portable 'Kodak' camera, which he sold by the thousand with the slogan *You press the button and we do the rest*.

Before 1907, cameras only took black and white pictures. If people wanted colour photographs they had to colour them by hand. French brothers Auguste and Louis Lumière introduced the first successful colour photography in 1907. It used a colour screen that was coated in a chemical which was sensitive to all colours.

Researchers were still trying to improve the colour photography process and in 1935 two American musicians, Leopld Godowsky and Leopold Mannes did just that. Their invention of the Kodachrome film, which was suitable for projection and reproduction, led the way into the modern era of photography.

Early cameras were simple boxes. This one was made in 1850. An optician had made the lens especially for it.

14

Technology has allowed enormous developments in the processes used in photography. Colour photography is now considered to be standard.

In 1972, a camera was invented by Polaroid which allowed instant colour prints to be produced in less than a minute. The camera ejects a piece of film on paper immediately after the picture has been taken.

In 1990 Kodak introduced PhotoCD which converts normal film into a digital form and stores them on a compact disc for viewing on a computer or television.

Today, technology exists which allows an image to be stored **digitally** rather than on a piece of film. A camera stores the picture as a series of codes. Each code represents one coloured dot or pixel on the picture. Each picture can be made up of millions of pixels. A digital image can be stored on a computer, or easily sent via e-mail to friends and family.

There is a small computer chip inside a digital camera which stores the image digitally.

THE MOVIES

The Movies

Since 1900 technological advances in photography made the development of moving pictures possible. The cinema and the movie industry was born, introducing people to a whole new world of entertainment and information.

Who invented movies?

In 1894, Thomas Edison, the American inventor who developed the first light bulb and the record player, invented a new machine called a Kinetoscope. This showed moving pictures, but only one person could watch it, through a small eyepiece.

At the same time in France, a scientist called Etienne Jules Marey built a movie camera and a projector. He could record and then project people and animals moving in slow motion.

In France, the Lumière brothers, Auguste and Louis, were working on a movie camera and a projector. They made the first proper movie (a few minutes rather than a few seconds long) and opened the world's first public theatres for watching movies in 1895 – the Cinematograph and the Biograph. In 1896, Edison also managed to project his films using what he called a Vitascope.

This is a 'frame' (a single photographic image) from the film *'L'arrive d'un train en gare'* (the arrival of a train in a station). The quick succession of photographs would have made it look like the train was moving into the station.

Losing the 'flickers'

Early movies were filmed and projected by turning a handle at 16 frames a second. This gave a jerky, flickery, movement – many people called early movies 'the flickers'. Once movies were seen as profitable, companies competed to produce equipment that took film faster and more smoothly. Modern film is shot at 24 frames a second. It is shot and replayed mechanically, for the smoothest possible effect.

Effects on film

The first colour film was hand tinted. But technicians in the movie industry soon produced colour film. From 1913 they used layers of film for special effects, this is called back projection. Actors are filmed against a plain background. Then an exciting background is filmed and the actors' images from the first film are shot against this. At first back projection was used for things like car chases, so that the actors did not really have to drive. Now it is used to show space, and to mix cartoons and real action.

Now that film can be **digitized** all sorts of strange transformations can be done on screen.

Who framed Roger Rabbit? used special effects to combine real people and cartoons together on film.

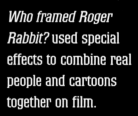

Technological toys

In 1900 toys used simple technology. Clockwork toys were very popular. Children could also compete with each other to catch the most magnetic fish or ducks on poles with magnets on the end. Some expensive toy trains and boats even worked on real steam power. But most of the time children played card games or ball games.

Board games were also a popular form of entertainment. This one was made in 1827.

A different world

Children in 1900 could enter imaginary worlds by reading about them. They could also create these worlds by dressing up play.

The most technologically advanced way to create these worlds was to use toy theatres. These came as kits. The simplest kits just had cardboard cut-out pieces to build the stage and characters, which were moved onto the stage clipped into wires. The most complicated had trapdoors that could be worked by levers and oil lamps to light the stage.

Computer fun

The development of the **laser**, the **silicon chip** and the microprocessor has made a whole new world of **electronic**, computer-controlled entertainment possible.

Computer games

When computer technology became more compact and cheaper in the 1970s, it was used to develop toys and games. Today, there are computer games that you can play in purpose-built games arcades, games systems that you play using a television screen, and hand-held video games powered by batteries.

Blistered thumbs

Games consoles that use televisions screens can be played by one or two players. Each player needs a control called a joypad, which you hold in your hands and operate using both thumbs. The joypad lets the player change direction on the screen.

Virtual reality pets

The late 1990s saw a craze develop for virtual reality pets. These are small, battery powered hand-held video games that have been programmed to mimic the life of a pet and its needs for such things as sleep, food and attention. The pet's 'owner' has to satisfy these to keep the pet 'alive'.

Virtual reality worlds

In 1900, children might play at being knights by dressing up with buckets on their heads and waving sticks as swords. Today, using a virtual reality headset, it is possible to enter into the world of a medieval knight. By wearing a headset and special gloves, a person can actually seem to be part of what is going on in a computer program. This realistic type of computer game can be used for fun or education – or even both!

The virtual reality headset and data glove contain a sensor that allows the computer to calculate the way the person is looking and so what they can see.

In 1900 the only way of investigating space was the same as it had been since 1608 – by using a telescope.

How telescopes work

Telescopes in 1900 worked by using a combination of a convex (curved out) lens and a concave (curved in) eyepiece lens. Light reflecting off the convex lens on to the concave lens magnifies the object being observed. The larger the convex lens, the greater the magnification.

Bigger and better

The very first telescopes had lenses that were only a few inches across. By 1900 a US company was grinding lenses that were just over one metre across. One of these was used in 1897 when the Yerkes Observatory opened in Wisconsin in the USA. But a different system, first proposed by English scientist Isaac Newton in 1671, was gaining popularity.

This system uses a curved mirror instead of the convex lens, and a flat mirror positioned at a 45° angle to reflect the object observed into the eyepiece.

To begin with these reflecting telescopes could only focus on a small part of the sky because they were difficult to move. By 1917, when the huge 2.5 metre reflecting telescope opened at the Mount Wilson Observatory in California, these mechanical problems had been solved.

The telescope was the only way of investigating space in the 1900s. This one was made in 1884 in Dublin.

Powerful telescopes

Professional astronomers and amateur star-gazers still use telescopes with a similar design to those in 1900. But there is now a new kind of telescope that takes advantage of all the advances in **electronics**, photography and computer science – the radio telescope. It does not work by catching the light from stars and planets, instead it picks up sound waves. It looks more like a giant aerial in a curved dish than a telescope. Since all sound has **wavelengths**, the sound can be used to recreate the shapes 'seen' by the telescope, but it can also do much more than an optical telescope. For example, radio telescopes can tell us what the rings of the planet Saturn are made of, by picking up the sound waves.

Radio telescopes have led to a whole world of invisible astronomy. By picking up other things invisible to the human eye, such as gamma rays and ultraviolet radiation, we are able to learn more about the universe.

Studying space

Another development since 1900 is the use of telescopes that are outside the Earth's atmosphere. Telescopes in space are free of any interference from the Earth's atmosphere. Also, they are not affected by the growing problem of light **pollution** from towns and cities around the world. Some of the most effective telescopes on the Earth's surface today are sited in remote places, like the deserts of northern Chile and the Canary Islands, away from light pollution.

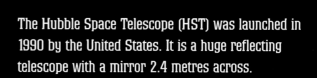

The Hubble Space Telescope (HST) was launched in 1990 by the United States. It is a huge reflecting telescope with a mirror 2.4 metres across.

In 1900 people could study space through telescopes. There were books available about the stars and planets, and there were star charts. But nobody had ever been in space. Scientists could only think about travelling there. The Wright brothers' first aeroplane flight was not until 1903, and there were even parts of the Earth that were still unexplored, such as Antarctica.

How to get there

The main problem of travelling into space was creating enough power to escape the Earth's gravity. Because most early engines had been steam powered, one idea was that spaceships would have to be steam driven too, and carry huge amounts of heavy, bulky coal. But this would make a spacecraft too big.

Another idea was that gunpowder could be used to fire a rocket into space, but again there was the problem of creating enough thrust for the rocket to escape the Earth's gravity.

New, liquid fuel

The invention of a motor car with an **internal combustion engine** in 1881 by German Karl Benz brought a new fuel into use – petrol. Petrol was lighter and took up less space. Scientists, like Konstantin Tsiolkovsky (1857-1935) in Russia, began to wonder whether it was possible to blast a rocket out of the Earth's gravitational pull using petrol as a fuel. Karl Benz developed theories of combining liquid fuels and igniting them so that they would expand as a jet of gas to provide enough thrust.

This is a rare photograph of Tsiolkovsky in his study with a model of his rocket.

The space race

From 1900 to the first successful launch of a manned spacecraft in 1961, the technology needed to escape the Earth and explore space developed. Only twelve years after the Russians first successful launch of a satellite (*Sputnik 1*) in 1957, US astronauts Armstrong and Aldrin walked on the surface of the Moon and returned to tell their story.

One of the things that pushed space exploration along was the competition between the USA and the Soviet Union (now Russia) to succeed in what became known as the space race. Each country spent huge amounts of money and hired the best scientists in their countries. They were afraid that which ever country controlled space would control the world.

Progressing, not racing

Although the space race is now over and astronauts from Russia, the USA and other countries have joined together to form crews for space missions, there are still many unexplored space frontiers.

Orbiting space stations like the *Skylab* and *Mir* have meant that astronauts can live and work in space for longer periods. But to discover more about distant objects in space unmanned **space probes** have been the only practical method. The great distances make journey times too long for crewed missions. For example, it took the *Voyager 2* probe from 1977 to 1989 to travel from Earth to the edge of our Solar System.

Today's technology allows humans to 'walk' in space using a special suit and backpack which provides them with the air needed to survive and seals them off from the vacuum of space.

STAYING IN SPACE

In 1900, the idea of going into space seemed almost impossible. The problems of staying in space for any length of time seemed insoluble. How could a space traveller survive in the vacuum of space without air to breathe?

Taking or making air

Air could be put into containers and taken into space, but the containers would be too heavy and bulky. The other obvious answer was to make air while in space. The Russian scientist Tsiolkovsky suggested taking plants into space. Plants had two advantages – they made oxygen during photosynthesis, and they made it by taking in carbon dioxide, the waste air people breathe out.

Tsiolkovsky's old house is now a museum. This is a display of his work on rocket-engineering.

Tsiolkovsky thought that taking enough of the right plants would allow people to stay in space for as long as they wished.

Zero gravity

Outside of the gravitational pull of the Earth and other bodies in space there is no gravity. This condition of zero gravity can cause many problems, such as the need to keep objects secure. Even a drink floats up out of a cup, and it is impossible to pour! The crew are in a state of continual weightlessness. In 1900, scientists were so preoccupied with getting into space that they never really worried about many of the physical problems astronauts would face. Even Tsiolkovsky did not think about the fact that his plants would have been floating about inside his space station.

Space stations

Today, modern space stations are assembled in orbit and have room for astronauts to eat, sleep and carry out experiments.

The first Soviet space station, *Salyut 1*, was launched in 1971 and the first US station, *Skylab*, two years later. The Soviet-launched *Mir* space station, which has been visited and used by astronauts from different countries, was in use from 1986 to 1998. It used the rays of the sun to provide its energy and received regular supplies from Earth.

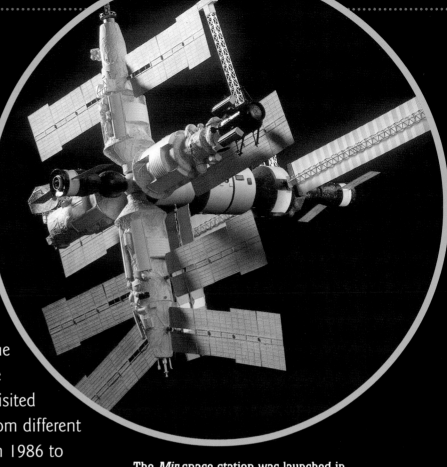

The *Mir* space station was launched in stages between 1986–1966. This is a model of the completed station.

The reusable Shuttle

The high cost of building spacecraft that could only go on one mission made the USA develop a space vehicle that could go into space and come back to Earth over and over again. In 1981, the first Space Shuttle, *Columbia*, was launched and successfully returned to Earth at the end of its mission.

The various members of the shuttle fleet are protected from the intense heat of re-entry into the Earth's atmosphere by special heat-proof tiles. The winged-shape of the shuttles meant they can glide down to Earth at the end of a mission, like a plane, rather than fall to the ground or into the sea with only a parachute.

In 1900, exploring the other planets of our Solar System was seen as a subject suitable for **science fiction**. Frenchman Jules Verne wrote the first science fiction story, *From the Earth to the Moon*, in 1865. In the book, his space travellers are shot into space from a giant gun.

One man's view

The Englishman H. G. Wells wrote *First Men on the Moon* in 1901. Before writing this novel, Wells researched the known facts about space and the Moon.

Well's space travellers, Bedford and Cavor, reach the Moon by discovering a mysterious power source, known only to Cavor. When they arrive on the Moon they find that they can breathe the air and that because of the zero gravity, they can bound around. The Moon is inhabited by aliens who lived under the Moon's surface. The travellers get separated and Bedford returns to Earth without Cavor. Cavor is captured by the aliens, learns to talk to the creatures and sends messages back to Earth, describing the way the aliens live. He also tells the aliens about the lifestyle of human beings, including their war-like tendencies throughout history. The aliens then kill him to stop other humans reaching the Moon.

This is an illustration from the book by H.G. Wells. This is what he thought the inhabitants of the Moon would look like.

No aliens!

On 20 July 1969, US astronauts Neil Armstrong and Buzz Aldrin stepped onto the surface of the Moon, but there were no aliens there to greet them. Their experience was very different from that imagined by Wells. They did, however, bound about in the zero gravity, but they could not breathe without the help of the oxygen in their spacesuits. They found no signs of life.

This is a pictue of Jupiter's Great Red Spot region taken from *Voyager 2*.

Visiting other planets

The Moon is the only place in space that people have been able to visit so far. Unmanned **space probes** have examined all of the planets in our Solar System with the exception of Pluto. In 1997, the US *Pathfinder* probe landed on the surface of Mars. It used a small roving four-wheeled vehicle, the *Sojourner*, to explore the surface, sending back information about the landscape, while *Pathfinder* took photographs and relayed them to mission control on Earth. A crewed mission to Mars is planned for early in the next century.

Discovering the Solar System's secrets

Since the 1960s, telescopes and unmanned probes have revealed more and more about the Solar System and the planets, moons, asteroids and comets in it. Radio telescopes show the geology of the various heavenly bodies. Unmanned space probes have photographed and even landed on planets to send back detailed information about their temperatures, atmospheres and the likelihood of astronauts ever being able to land there.

As technology develops, people will be able to explore deeper into space, with unmanned **space probes**, telescopes and, hopefully, crewed missions.

Rapid colonization

Michio Kaku, Physics Professor at the City University of New York and author of *Visions*, suggests that people will want to begin rapidly colonizing other planets, for one very good reason: '*One of the main forces driving us to colonize other planets is the fear of planetary collapse – that we will no longer be able to live on Earth. The disintegration of the ozone layer, which will continue to lead to all kinds of environmental problems, driven by* **fossil fuel** *consumption* **polluting** *the atmosphere. So many nations are dependent on fossil fuels that consumption will continue to rise in the 21st century and continue to disrupt the world's weather and ecology.*'

Earth, no longer home

The future studies project, Perspectives 2100, suggested on the Internet that humans will be living in space by the middle of the 21st century: '*These space colonies will be inside giant spheres, rings or cylinders constructed in space, using resources from planets other than Earth. The people inside will recycle air, water and waste, creating an environment that looks very like Earth, with lakes, rivers, hills and trees as well as homes and work places.*'

In 1995 the spacecraft *Galileo* released an unmanned probe to take measurements of Jupiter's atmosphere. This is an artist's impression of the probe's release.

Living in space

The discovery of water on the Moon in 1998 was especially exciting because it opens up the possibility of using the Moon as a base for the exploration of other planets, or even as a site for a permanent space station.

Probes confirmed that the far side of the Moon, which is never in sunlight, had lakes of frozen water. This means it would be possible to have permanent space stations on the Moon as there would be a supply of water for drinking and growing food. The water would also be useful for refuelling spacecraft that were carrying on further into space.

Living on the Moon

Richard Taylor of the British Interplanetary Society points out in *The Sunday Times* that living quarters on the Moon would have to be underground. There would be a difference between visiting space and living there full-time: '*Bubble cities (cities under clear domes) would only work so long as you don't spend too much time in them, due to the radiation. Structures where people live permanently would have to be built underground.*'

These lunar water maps show water is in the upper 50cm of soil on the Moon's surface. Pink and purple show a large amount of water is present. Red and yellow show small amounts of water. The Moon's northern hemisphere is shown on the left, the southern one is on the right.

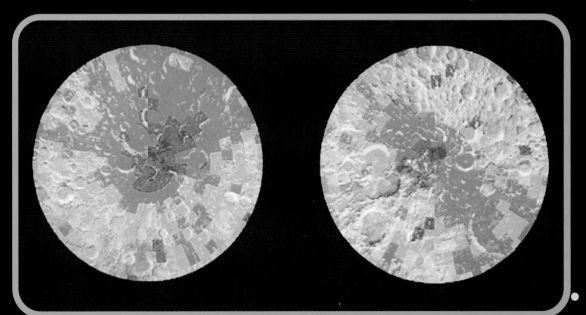

alternating current (AC) an electric current where the electricity moves backwards and forwards all the time

assembly line a system where workers line up along a conveyor belt and all do one small job making a product, for instance a car, which moves along the conveyor belt from worker to worker

by-product any thing or effect which is produced during another process or by an event

capacitor a device for storing electricity

census an official count of the inhabitants of a country

conductor a material which allows an electric current to pass through it easily

developed/developing countries developed countries, such as the USA, are rich, industrial countries. Developing countries began industrialization later, have less industry and are not as rich.

digital a system of 1s and 0s, used to send and store information. Digital images are stored on computers as a series of dots.

direct current (DC) an electric current where the electricity is always moving in the same direction

electronic using electricity to provide power

fossil fuel fuels like coal, formed from the remains of prehistoric plants and animals that are dug out of the ground

frequency the level at which a sound is pitched, or how often it repeats in a second

generator a machine that produces energy from fuel

hydro-electric power electricity made by using water power

internal combustion engine an engine that works by producing a controlled explosion inside the engine which produces gases that power the engine

lasers a device that produces a thin, fierce, beam of light that can be used at different levels to burn a hole through steel, perform operations of play CDs

mechanized a system that is mechanized has at least part of the work done by machines

nuclear power power produced by making a controlled atomic explosion in a specially designed power station

pharmaceuticals medicines

pollution dirt and waste that is put into the air or water and make it harmful to use

radioactive something that produces tiny particles or waves that can damage living cells. Some nuclear waste, produced when nuclear power is generated, is radioactive.

renewable something that can replace itself, or can be replaced

science fiction stories made up about the future or some other time that use imagined scientific discoveries to create their worlds

silicon chip a small piece of silicon that store and process electric signals

space probes radio controlled, unmanned, spacecraft that are sent into space to explore planets that manned spacecraft could never reach

telegraph messages sent by using electrical signals beamed along a wire above or below ground

wavelengths the length of time it takes for a single wave to form. Radio wavelengths can be long, medium or short.

INDEX